W9-BPL-179

Harriet Ziefert

ROCKHEADS

Illustrated by Todd McKie

HOUGHTON MIFFLIN COMPANY BOSTON 2004

Walter Lorraine Books

For Judy
—T.M.

For Jen Ziefert, who put
all the pieces together
—H.Z.

Walter Lorraine *wr* Books

Text copyright © 2004 by Harriet Ziefert
Illustrations copyright © 2004 by Todd McKie
All rights reserved. For information about permission
to reproduce selections from this book, write to
Permissions, Houghton Mifflin Company,
215 Park Avenue South, New York, New York 10003.

www.houghtonmifflinbooks.com

Library of Congress Cataloging-in-Publication Data

Ziefert, Harriet.
Rockheads / by Harriet Ziefert ; illustrations by Todd McKie.
p. cm.
Summary: Introduces counting and basic addition, as shown through
activities that involve specific numbers of participants, such as a
musical quartet and nine players on a Little League team.
ISBN 0-618-34574-4
1. Counting—Juvenile literature. 2. Addition—Juvenile literature.
[1. Counting. 2. Addition.] I. McKie, Todd, 1944– ill. II. Title.
QA113.Z56 2004
513.2'11—dc22
2003014795

Printed in China for Harriet Ziefert, Inc.
1 3 5 7 9 10 8 6 4 2

Here I am. There's only one me.
I'm all alone, as you can see.

But when I'm with Blair,

We're two. We're a pair.

Now meet my friend Cleo.

We're three. We're a trio.

Now it's music with Seymour,

And we're a quartet of four.

Forwards, guards, and the center, Jean,

Five of us make a basketball team.

With Fred, a gymnast, in the group,

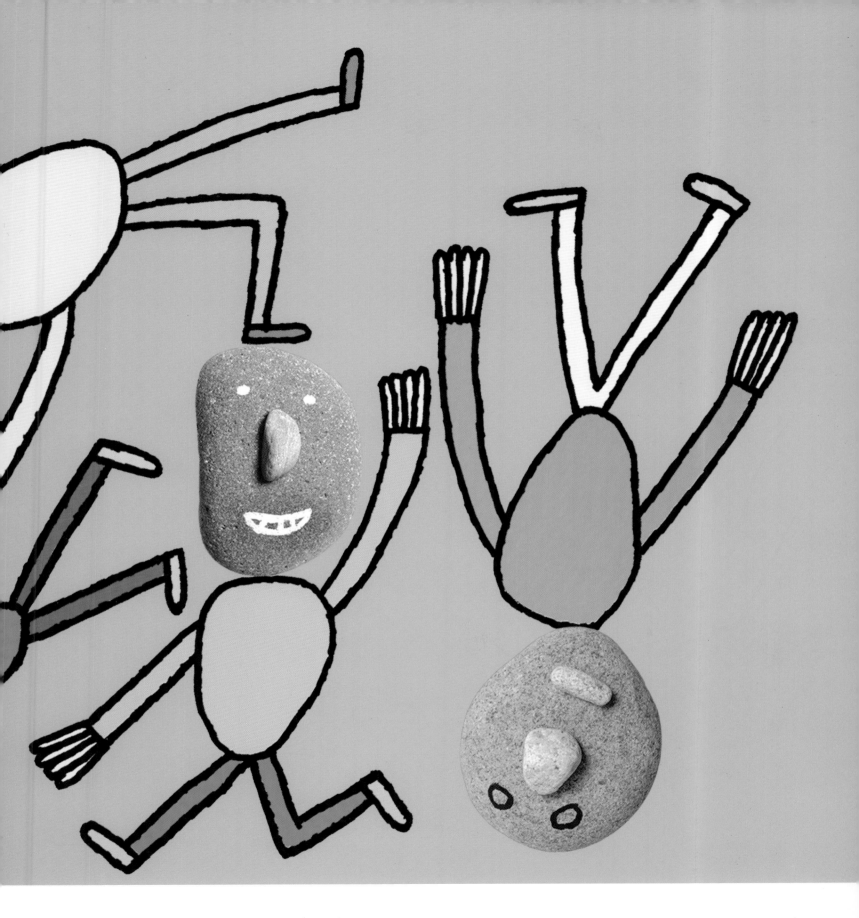

We're a six-kid acrobatic troop.

Listen up! On sax there's Devin.

That makes us a band of seven.

An octet is a group of eight.

Low notes are by baritone, Nate.

Infielders, outfielders, and the pitcher, Stine,

Make us a Little League team of nine.

Our cheerleading squad totals ten.

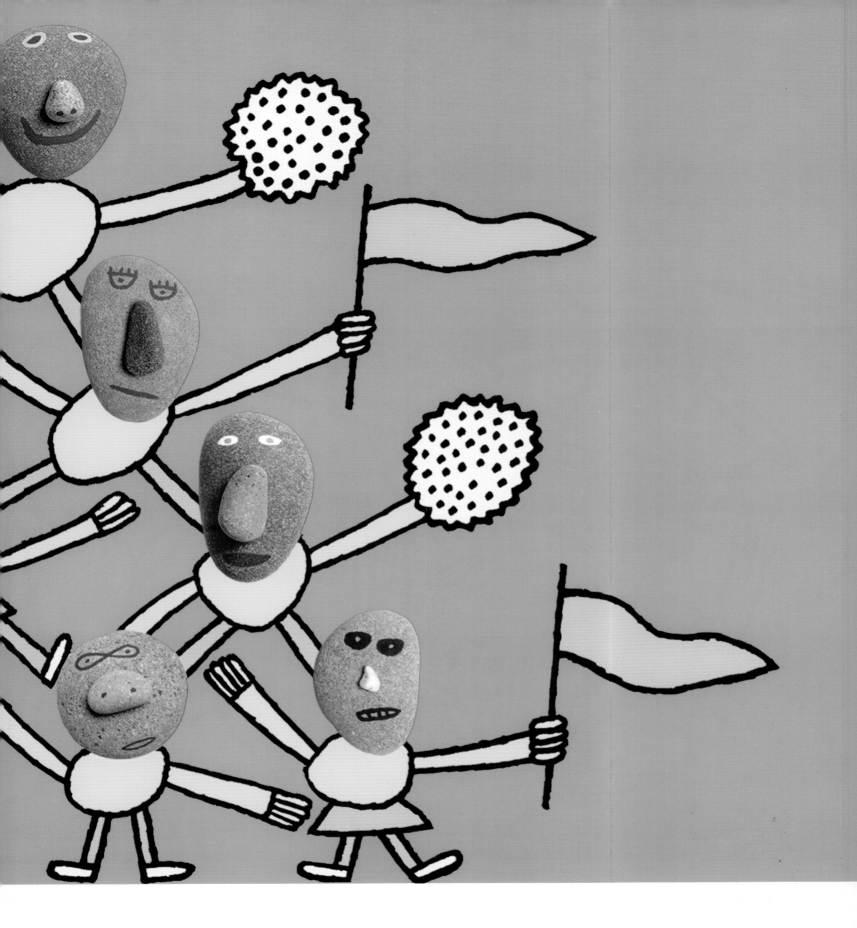

Can you guess which kid is Jen?

Eleven players on a soccer squad.

Ten on the field plus the goalie, Todd.

Twelve kids make an even dozen.

The last to join is Cleo's cousin.

Everyone's gone, and there's only me.
What do you think my name should be?

Illustrator's Note

I've collected beach stones for many years, and for the past three years I've been turning them into sculptures. I keep the sculptures simple — serious faces, funny faces, faces with quizzical expressions, startled expressions, dopey expressions, smart expressions. A gamut, I guess, of human emotions expressed in stone and paint and industrial epoxy.

I really enjoy making the sculptures. But accidents do happen, and stones are heavy. I've dropped stones on my toes. I've tripped over them. I've hurt my back hauling them around.

One time I slipped on a wet rock on a beach in Maine and knocked myself out. When I woke up, I thought I'd gone blind, but then I realized it was just the blood flowing into my eyes. After applying pressure to the cut and going to the hospital and getting stitched up, I was almost as good as new again.

Oh, friends, what we do for our art!

—T.M.

HOW MANY ROCKHEADS CAN YOU FIND?

STINE
Find 6

TODD
Find 5

CLEO
Find 13

BLAIR
Find 14

CLEO'S COUSIN
Find 3

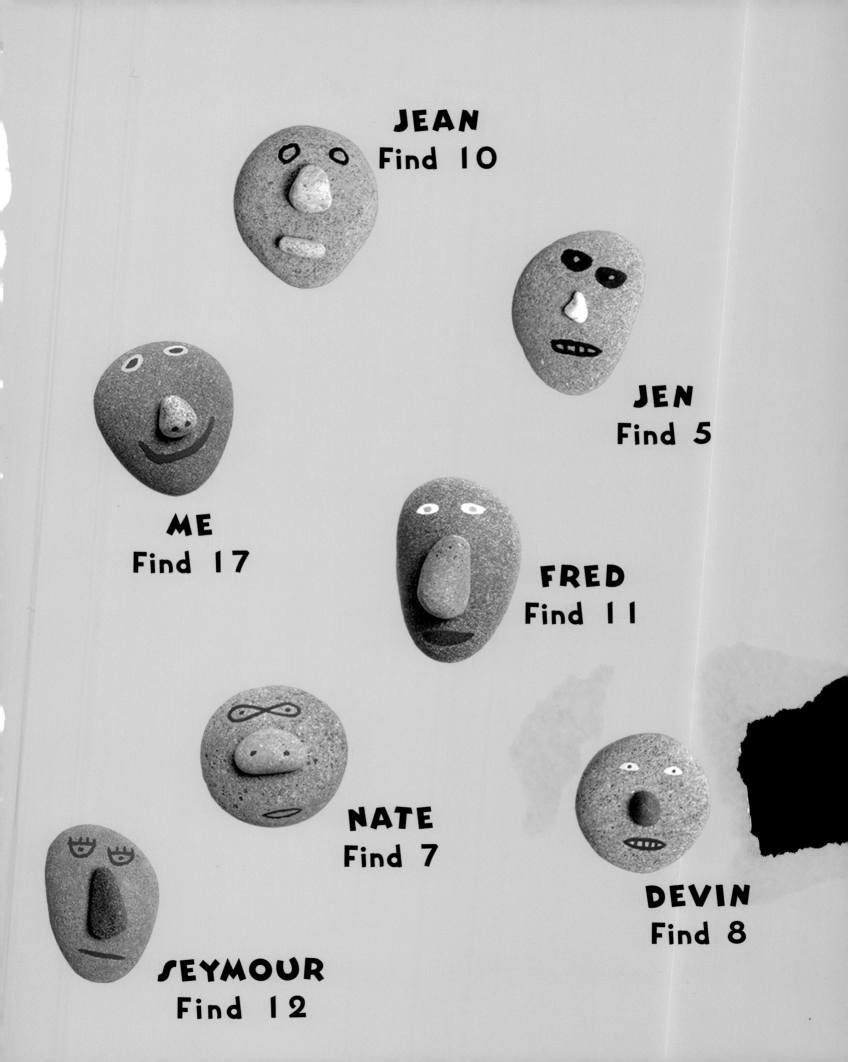

JEAN
Find 10

JEN
Find 5

ME
Find 17

FRED
Find 11

NATE
Find 7

DEVIN
Find 8

SEYMOUR
Find 12